Encounters

Encounters

Poems about Race, Ethnicity and Identity

Paula Cole Jones, EDITOR

Skinner House Books

Boston

Printed in the United States

Cover design by Suzanne Morgan
Cover art "Tethered/Free" © 2004 Eleanor Rubin, http://ellyrubinjournal
    .typepad.com
Text design by Jeff Miller

ISBN 1-55896-574-2
978-1-55896-574-4

13 12 11 10
6 5 4 3 2 1

Library of Congress Cataloging-in-Publication Data

Encounters : poems about race, ethnicity and identity / Paula Cole Jones, editor.
        p. cm.
    ISBN-13: 978-1-55896-574-4 (pbk. : alk. paper)
    ISBN-10: 1-55896-574-2 (pbk. : alk. paper)
    1. American poetry—21st century.   2. Race relations—Poetry.   I. Cole Jones,
Paula.
    PS595.R32E53 2010
    811'.6093529—dc22

                                                                    2010031271

Copyright acknowledgments are on pages 161–162.

Contents

Foreword

Race is so very hard for our parents and loved ones to talk about openly, so we encounter it when least prepared. It is as if we are walking about with our eyes wide shut and then this idea of race intrudes like a bolt of lightning. In the aftermath of our epiphany, things are never the same. The jolt rearranges our thinking—the searing pain seems without end. We never completely heal from the experience, but the initial discordant notes are reassembled in our minds and hearts as the blues. We survive and cope, and seek out others to share our new insights. Some, like the voices in this volume, write poems about racial encounters. Their phrasing, juxtapositions, interrogations, and wordsmith become like touchstones—so that when the next encounter with race tries to ruin a perfectly beautiful day, we may well reach for this little book of poems and find the one that brings relief and captures the moment.

At its core, racism is about stigma, and when one group has power over others, it is possible to racialize and stigmatize just about *any* group. Consequently, the poems in this volume were written by all manner of folk—black, white, brown, and yellow.

Because our eyes look "outward," we are mostly unaware of how we look. It is only through the eyes and actions of others that we see ourselves. That someone might recoil at the mere sight of our differentness always comes as a surprise. Hours before, we stepped out of the shower and rather enjoyed the lips, skin, and hair we saw reflected in the mirror. We dressed and might even have felt stylish as we closed the door of our residence and stepped out to meet the world. Now this clerk, this idiot, responds with apoplexy when, rather than place the money on the counter, we place it in her hand, causing our skin to touch. Touching should signal the linking of our humanity, but racial schemas can denude and eviscerate those connections, leading to relationships marked by evil. In this racial scenario, the players can switch roles, and sometimes it is the black person trying to avoid the touch of a white person, and in another version, it is the white person trying to avoid contact with a black hand. It is in the aftermath of such encounters that we can reach for this text, assembled for us by Paula Cole Jones.

Soul musician Billy Paul said it best in his song about another Mrs. Jones. After reading these poems of such healing power and insight, you are likely to join me in singing that chorus, "Me and Mrs. Jones have a thing going on."

—*William E. Cross, Jr., Ph.D., author of* Shades of Black

Preface

The poets in this book know collectively what each of us alone cannot know. In a chorus of voices they make public what lies in the gap between our ideals and the limitations of our humanity. These artists speak the silent messages that swirl between self and other in the intimate spaces of our identities. They help us remember what we have been taught to ignore. To know their poems is to carry the human story in our own hearts.

In the summer of 1992 I packed twenty-two rolls of film and a hardback journal for a vacation to Egypt. I had spent months reading and listening to scholars talk about the Great Nile civilization, but nothing could have prepared me for this trip.

To this day, I easily remember the rhythmic clack and sway of the overnight train south from Cairo to Aswan, the elegant silhouettes of mosques against evening orange horizons on the Nile River, and bumpy camel rides along dusty roads. But, it was the Temple of Luxor that pierced my soul. I stood dwarfed between rows of towering granite columns, scribbling in my journal. My friend Roland nudged my arm, pointed a slim finger, and said, "Look." Speechless, I stared at a monument against the cloudless sky. An obelisk, thousands of years old, pointed upward among the Egyptian ruins. Instantly spliced in my mind was an image of the Washington Monument. I had read that the monument was designed by a French architect. How could I not have known that the Washington Monument was a modern version of African architecture? The original designers, architects in ancient

Africa, had not been acknowledged. I had to travel around the globe to learn this truth first hand.

For me the obelisk symbolized American miseducation about African civilization—and ultimately about race. Eight months before traveling to Egypt, I held in my hands small iron shackles recovered from the slave ship *Henrietta Marie*, which sank off of Key West. With a young daughter at home, knowing that these shackles once bound someone's child, I felt my eyes fill with tears and I said, "How in the world could anyone have allowed this to happen?" New examinations about the enslavement of African people and ancient African history changed my life. I returned from Egypt angry and frustrated. I began to look at literature differently. I poured through my daughter's picture books to see what messages had been conveyed in our innocent, intimate moments of sharing stories together. Back in the United States and safe in my community, I avoided contact with European Americans because I had to work things out. I immersed myself further in the history of being black in America and part of the African Diaspora. This provided me with a new and more expansive narrative that I could trust.

I felt a strong need to capture these feelings and insights in a poem. Writing can release the tension between ambiguous contradiction and personal resolve. It took me a year to work the emotions into verse.

Each poem in this collection has its own story about why and how it was written and what it conveys. Words cannot tell the whole tale. These poems are meant to be heard, seen and felt. They are like time capsules, containing images and energy waiting to be released by us, the readers. As we digest their contents, we discover what is on our own hearts and minds.

Toni Morrison once said, "If there's a book you really want to read but it hasn't been written yet, then you must write it." Having conducted hundreds of discussions on racism, ethnicity, identity and social change, I have longed for a book like this one—presenting a wide range of voices that share insights about navigating this realm of culture. We must break the silence on how race and ethnicity are used to stereotype people. Only then can we truly encounter one another beyond superficialities and our own limited beliefs about humanity. I invite you into the conversation.

COUNTEE CULLEN

Near White

Ambiguous of race they stand
    By one disowned, scorned of another,
Not knowing where to stretch a hand,
    And cry, "My sister" or "My brother."

A. VAN JORDAN

Question

A brother offended is harder to be won than a strong city,
and their contentions are like the bars of a castle.

—*Proverbs* 18:19

What up, brother? The white teen with dreadlocks
    and a confederate flag tattoo on his arm asks,
and the black man to whom the question is addressed
    seems pensive: He may teach college or fix cars,

but right now he's a philosopher weighing an answer;
    he's survived his first year in the south, but he always
expected love and hate to speak clearer
    on red soil. Dreadlocks and a confederate flag?

What message crossed in the mind of this young man?
    Did he start to listen to reggae after the tattoo?
The nanosecond freezes before they pass each other
    on this street corner in downtown Asheville, North

Carolina, which allows enough time for him to remember
    the last time he had seen a confederate flag
so out of place. He was driving a Uhaul truck
    down I-71 in Ohio when, to his surprise, as he approached

Cincinnati, he saw the largest confederate flag of his life painted
    on the roof of a barn. In Ohio, where slaves escaped to find

2

freedom, a confederate flag? A flag of secession, of blood and bone,
    of black against white, of homeland fighting homeland, of fear

of unity; the belief that blacks lacked spirit and heart; the grief
    of loss and longing; fear of shackle and whip; hatred so deep
that it pitted him against his own brother; hatred so deep it made
    him gnaw off his own white hand; turned lovers into soldiers,

into wielders of guns and bayonets and bottles and stones—
    this flag, this birthmark of an endless struggle to conquer
and enslave and betray—to betray himself—yet holds, for all its
    pain, something worth pride in his white mind? The black wonders

if dreadlocks can make a white boy a minority in his own country.
    What up, brother? Of that abrupt question—from salutation
to spitting in each other's face, to looking into each other's eyes,
    to not shaking each other's hand, to weeping at each other's

history, to killing and forgiving and loving and enduring and enduring,
    of that abrupt question, and these transitions, and that electric
current sent to the brain and the heart and the tongue and the spine
    and the bowels, raising up one more remnant of history—nothing

remains as clear as the laughing wind that brushes his face when
    he hears brother slip from between the teeth of a contemporary
confederate. *What up, brother?* The white asks the black, who
    decides to say nothing, verbally, but stands and stares into these blue

eyes, as if he were the one who asked the question, like a sphinx
    tripping up a fool with the wrong answer to another tragic riddle.

Being Jewish in a Small Town

Someone writes kike on
the blackboard and the
"k's" pull thru the
chalk   stick in my

plump pale thighs
even after the high
school burns down the
word is written in

the ashes   my under
pants elastic snaps
on Main St because
I can't go to

Pilgrim Fellowship
I'm the one Jewish girl
in town but the 4
Cohen brothers

want blond hair
blowing from their
car   they don't know
my black braids

smell of almond
I wear my clothes
loose so no one
dreams who I am

will never know
Hebrew   keep a
Christmas tree in
my drawer   in

the dark   my fingers
could be the menorah
that pulls you toward
honey in the snow

NELLIE WONG

Can't Tell

When World War II was declared
on the morning radio,
we glued our ears, widened our eyes.
Our bodies shivered.

A voice said
Japan was the enemy,
Pearl Harbor a shambles
and in our grocery store
in Berkeley, we were suspended
next to the meat market
where voices hummed,
valises, pots and pans packed,
no more hot dogs, baloney,
pork kidneys.

We children huddled on wooden planks
and my parents whispered:
We are Chinese, we are Chinese.
Safety pins anchored,
our loins ached.

Shortly our Japanese neighbors vanished
and my parents continued to whisper:
We are Chinese, we are Chinese.

We wore black arm bands,
put up a sign
in bold letters.

Cincinnati

Freedom at last
in this town aimless
I walked against the rush
hour traffic
My first day
in a real city
where

no one knew me.

No one except one
hissing voice that said
dirty jap
warm spittle on my right cheek.
I turned and faced
the shop window
and my spittled face
spilled onto a hill
of books.
Words on display.

In Government Square
people criss-crossed
the street
like the spokes of
a giant wheel.

I lifted my right hand
but it would not obey me.
My other hand fumbled
for a hankie.
My tears would not
wash it. They stopped
and parted.
My hankie brushed
the forked
tears and spittle
together.
I edged toward the curb
loosened my fisthold
and the bleached laced
mother-ironed hankie blossomed in
the gutter atop teeth marked
gum wads and heeled candy wrappers.

Everyone knew me.

Dance of the Letters

My father, in a 1956 gray suit,
had the jungle in his tie,
a macaw on Kelly green.
But today is Saturday, no briefs
to prepare, and he's in a T-shirt.

I sit on his lap with my *ABC*
Golden Book, and he orders the letters
to dance. The *A* prancing red
as an apple, the *E* a lumbering elephant,
the *C* chased by the *D* while the sly *F*

is snickering in his russet fur coat.
My mother says my breakthrough
was the *M* somersaulting into a *W*.
Not a mouse transformed into a wallaby
at all, but sounds that we can see.

Later, my father trots me out
to the living room like a trained *Z*.
Not yet four, I read newspaper headlines
out loud for Tito Juanito and Tita Naty
or for anyone who drops in.

Six years later, I am that boy
in a black Giants cap, intertwining orange

letters S and F, carrying my father's
forgotten lunch to the catacombs
of the UCSF Medical Center,

and I love the hallway cool before the swirling
heat from the Print Shop door.
In his inky apron, my father smiles,
but his eyes are tired. The night before,
I pulled the pillow over my head, while he
argued with my mother
till two a.m. about that old double bind:
a rule to keep American citizens from
practicing law in the Philippines.
His University of Manila

law degree made useless.
But California's just as bad.
"You can't work in your goddamn
profession stateside either!" he shouts.
"Some land of opportunity."

There in the shimmer of the Print Shop, I can't
understand his bitterness. I savor
the staccato sounds. He leans
into the noise of huge machines, putting
vowels and consonants into neat stacks.

The Best Conversation on Race

The best conversation on race that I've never had
would have started the time Walter Mudu called me a nigger.
Actually, that's not quite what he said.
Instead of passing the platter of sushi around the room
as my mother taught me to do as a child,
I stood there casually with the platter in my left hand,
systematically eating the entire thing with my right hand.
Aw, that's some nigger shit right there! Walter said.

The best conversation I never had on race
would have begun right there, but I don't quite know how.
Maybe I would have simply said, "Don't call me that."
Or, "I beg your pardon?"
Or even, "Bitch, tell me you didn't just say!"
Maybe I would have told him about the one time
I used the word myself and was sent to my room immediately.
The rest of *Roots* made little sense to me.
Why do they keep calling him Toby when his name is Kunta Kinté?

The conversation might have referenced the time,
long before Chris Rock, when a friend said,
*You know what I mean: there are black people and then there are
    niggers.*
And I told him that I did not know what he meant,
and would he please never use that word again in my presence.

It's so easy to climb up on a high horse when you're talking to white
    people.
Maybe that's why I never give them money on the street when they
    beg.

Once a black guy walking toward me
on the streets of Oakland threw his Styrofoam cup to the ground.
And you know what I said to him? Nothing.
Because I was afraid of getting shot or worse:
looking like a white guy telling a black guy what to do.
They say environmentalism is the activism of the privileged,
that you can afford to worry about the world
when you don't have to worry about yourself or your family.

I tell myself that the use of the word *nigger* by African America
is a strategy of reappropriation designed to disempower the word
the way feminists and homosexuals have done with *bitch* and *faggot*.
And since that strategy has effectively rid the world of all traces
of sexism and homophobia, I counter that the tactic is flawed
and like the President's war on Terror continues to create the problem
    it claims to fix.
Listen, I say: Your mother taught you to pass the sushi around,
but you stood there and ate it all yourself.
You disrespected your mother.
So maybe that's the "nigger shit" the brother
was accusing you of in the first place.

The truth is, it may have continued,
but the best conversation on race
isn't one you have with yourself.

13

Not Within Me

I can not help but look past the blackness of my skin,
past the flesh and blood cells,
past the working organs of my body—
I find there is no nigger within me.
only a man.
Though it may exist
the only evidence of its being
is the blackness printed on a white sheet
pressed between the covers
of my dictionary.

Passing

A professor invites me to his "Black Lit" class; they're
reading Larson's *Passing*. One of the black
students says, "Sometimes light-skinned blacks
think they can fool other blacks,
but *I* can always tell," looking
right through me.
After I tell them I am black,
I ask the class, "Was I passing
when I was just sitting here,
before I told you?" A white woman
shakes her head desperately, as if
I had deliberately deceived her.
She keeps examining my face,
then turning away
as if she hopes I'll disappear. Why presume
"passing" is based on what I leave out
and not what she fills in?
In one scene in the book, in a restaurant,
she's "passing,"
though no one checked her at the door—
"Hey, you black?"
My father, who looked white,
told this story: every year
when he'd go to get his driver's license,
the man at the window filling

out the form would ask,
"White or black?" pencil poised, without looking up.
My father wouldn't pass, but he might
use silence to trap a devil.
When he didn't speak, the man
would look up at my father's face.
"What do you think
he would always write?" my father'd say.

Waitress

They speak to you
in Spanish
to be funny
or in response to
your dark hair and eyes
and you answer in French
so they know
this is no ordinary
restaurant
but you laugh along
because they *are* funny
on vacation with their compadres
and they love the food
the drink
and you who bring it to them
and remember from last summer
a lime not a lemon
in their iced tea
or no salt on the margarita,
and for every one who asks
for your number
or comments on your dress
there are two who ask
what you are reading
or whether you have published

lately
and you are there with *your* compadres
dancing out an incredible ballet
of hot plates and crushed ice
until you go home
where your husband says
you smell like quesadillas
and he likes it
and your children
to whom checks mean nothing
squeal
as you empty your pockets
of all the gleaming coins
that they can count.

Foul Line—1987

Her back in a line straight
As an ironing board
She serves my lunch
And never shows her face
    My companion is right
    For her menu—white and male
    She gives him all her attention
    Reading his every wish
    With careful eyes as she avoids
    My gaze
Nothing personal
But all she sees is color
Black, a shadow, something dark
Near her left hip, the one she rests
Her elbow against when she wrist-
Flicks the plate dead center
On my placemat like a back-
Handed pitcher
    Such a little
    Gesture with all the effort
    Of breeding behind it
    So dainty, the proper flaunt
    Of a Southern girl's hanky
    And all within legal

If not civil limits
And I wonder vaguely if I might
Have met her in Selma
Or later opposite some other picket
Lines—we're the right age
For such encounters
    And despite laws to the contrary
    Neither of us has ever lost
    Our sense of misplacement
    And can say politely
    We both know how far we've come

ADRIAN C. LOUIS

Something About Being an Indian

There's something about being an Indian
we say to each other in a Bishop saloon
both of us forty with pony tails
grown down long to our Levi butts.
Yes, brother, it is the heart, and it is
the blood that we share.
The heart alone is not enough.

There's something about being an Indian
we say in soft whiskey voices that remember
many soft, brown women.
We laugh past the window and its vision
of constant traffic, the aimless yuppies
bound for the ski lodges.
Snow must be licentious for such fools:
white sheets to be soiled with temporal chill.
Yes, there's something about being an Indian
we say as we exit into the warmth
of Hell's secondary nature,
a place we call the Fire Water World.

The Men

What then shall we say to this?
If God is for us, who is against us?

—*Romans* 8:31

I
Today I saw black men
carrying babies,
pushing carriages,
holding their own.

II
Our streets filled
with good news,
we must write the
headlines ourselves.

III
When the world
makes a fist
we duck and counterpunch,
we jab and swing.

IV
Black men
at construction sites
lifting black earth,
black hearts, black
hands.

V
The young men
dress in black,
their clothes
just big enough
for love.

Poem for the Young White Man Who Asked Me How I, an Intelligent, Well-Read Person, Could Believe in the War Between Races

In my land there are no distinctions.
The barbed wire politics of oppression
have been torn down long ago. The only reminder
of past battles, lost or won, is a slight
rutting in the fertile fields.

In my land
people write poems about love,
full of nothing but contented childlike syllables.
Everyone reads Russian short stories and weeps.
There are no boundaries.
There is no hunger, no
complicated famine or greed.

I am not a revolutionary.
I don't even like political poems.
Do you think I can believe in a war between races?
I can deny it. I can forget about it
when I'm safe,
living on my own continent of harmony
and home, but I am not
there.

I believe in revolution
because everywhere the crosses are burning,
sharp-shooting goose-steppers round every corner,
there are snipers in the schools . . .
(I know you don't believe this.
You think this is nothing
but faddish exaggeration. But they
are not shooting at you.)

I'm marked by the color of my skin.
The bullets are discrete and designed to kill slowly.
They are aiming at my children.
These are facts.
Let me show you my wounds: my stumbling mind, my
"excuse me" tongue, and this
nagging preoccupation
with the feeling of not being good enough.

These bullets bury deeper than logic.
Racism is not intellectual.
I cannot reason these scars away.

Outside my door
there is a real enemy
who hates me.

I am a poet
who yearns to dance on rooftops,
to whisper delicate lines about joy
and the blessings of human understanding.

I try. I go to my land, my tower of words and
bolt the door, but the typewriter doesn't fade out
the sounds of blasting and muffled outrage.
My own days bring me slaps on the face.
Every day I am deluged with reminders
that this is not
my land

and this is my land.

I do not believe in the war between races

but in this country
there is war.

Floating Eden

When the Japanese bombed
American ships
the supplies
and the dead bodies
floated in the seas
surrounding the Philippines.

My father
and his friends
would swim out to
the cans of Spam
and the Hershey bars
and bring them back
to sandy shores.

These
tanned
skinny Asian boys
would hoard the corned beef hash
in secret places
in the woods
where they hid
from guerrillas.

"This," says my father,
"was how we developed a taste for America."

What Is Wrong?

What is wrong with me everywhere I go
No one seems to look at me.
    Sometimes I cry.

I walk through woods and sit on a stone.
I look at the stars and I sometimes wish.

Probably if my wish ever comes true,
Everyone will look at me.

*This poem was written in 1964 by a 12-year-old girl at the
Freedom School in Biloxi, Mississippi.*

what haunts him

that moment after the bartender
refused to serve the dark marine
and the three white skinned others
just sat there   that moment
before they rose and followed
their nappy brother
out into the USA they were
willing to die to defend
then

Patience

A lot of Black folk
Will use a
Black doctor/lawyer/dentist
Plumber/gardener/mechanic
Et cetera/et cetera
And have just one bad experience
Just one
And then never use another
Black doctor/lawyer/dentist/
Plumber/gardener/mechanic
Et cetera/et cetera
Again
Never again
But then
Black folk will use
An Arab doctor
A Jewish lawyer
A Japanese dentist
An Irish plumber
A Latino gardener
A Korean mechanic
Or a White/White
Et cetera/et cetera
And have

One/sometimes two/maybe three
Often four/even five
Do I hear six/
More like seven/okay eight
Bad experiences
And still go back
Again and again
And
Again and again
And
Again and again
And Black folk don't do that
Again and again
With each other
'Cause we're programmed with
A self-hating double standard
In which we only give each other
One chance/one try/one attempt/one opportunity
Just one
And only one
And sometimes
Not even one
And I wish we were a little
More patient with each other
At least
Just once

Immigrant Blues

People have been trying to kill me since I was born,
a man tells his son, trying to explain
the wisdom of learning a second tongue.

It's the same old story from the previous century
about my father and me.

The same old story from yesterday morning
about me and my son.

It's called "Survival Strategies
and the Melancholy of Racial Assimilation."

It's called "Psychological Paradigms of Displaced Persons,"

called "The Child Who'd Rather Play than Study."

Practice until you feel
the language inside you, says the man.

But what does he know about inside and outside,
my father who was spared nothing
in spite of the languages he used?

And me, confused about the flesh and soul,
who asked once into a telephone,
Am I inside you?

You're always inside me, a woman answered,
at peace with the body's finitude,
at peace with the soul's disregard
of space and time.

Am I inside you? I asked once
lying between her legs, confused
about the body and the heart.

If you don't believe you're inside me, you're not,
she answered, at peace with the body's greed,
at peace with the heart's bewilderment.

It's an ancient story from yesterday evening

called "Patterns of Love in Peoples of Diaspora,"

called "Loss of the Homeplace
and the Defilement of the Beloved,"

called "I Want to Sing but I Don't Know Any Songs."

Tattoo

My father won't talk about the numbers
3-7-8-2-5 between the wrist and elbow
blue as blood on his left forearm
Instead, he spreads himself over me
spilling his protection, like acid, until it burns
I wear him like a cloak, sweat under the weight

There were stories in the lines on his face
the nervous blue flash in his eyes
his bone-crushing hugs
I am drowning in his silence
trying to stay afloat on curiosity
Questions choke me and I swallow hard

We don't breathe the same air
speak the same language
live in the same universe
We are continents, worlds apart
I am sorry my life has remained unscathed
His scars still bleed, his bruises don't fade

If I could trade places with him
I would pad the rest of his days
wrap him in gauze and velvet
absorb the shocks and treat his wounds
I would scrub the numbers from his flesh
extinguish the fire and give him back his life

Race Relations

I sang in the sun
of my white oasis
as you broke stone

Then I sang and paraded
for the distant martyrs
loving the unknown

They lay still in the sun
of Sharpeville and Selma
while you broke stone

When you fled tyranny
face down in the street
signing stones with your blood

Far away I fell silent
in my white oasis
ringed with smoke and guns

Martyred in safety
I signed for lost causes
You bled on You bled on

Now I recommence singing
in a tentative voice
loving the known

I sing in the sun
and storm of the world
to the breakers of stone

You are sentenced to life
in the guilt of freedom
in the prison of memory

Haunted by brothers
who still break stone
I am sentenced to wait

And our love-hate duet
is drowned by the drum
of the breakers of stone

On the Subway

The young man and I face each other.
His feet are huge, in black sneakers
laced with white in a complex pattern like a
set of intentional scars. We are stuck on
opposite sides of the car, a couple of
molecules stuck in a rod of energy
rapidly moving through darkness. He has
or my white eye imagines he has
the casual cold look of a mugger,
alert under lowered eyelids. He is wearing
red, like the inside of the body
exposed. I am wearing old fur, the
whole skin of an animal taken
and used. I look at his unknown face,
he looks at my grandmother's coat, and I don't
know if I am in his power—
he could take my coat so easily, my
briefcase, my life—
or if he is in my power, the way I am
living off his life, eating the steak
he may not be eating, as if I am taking
the food from his mouth. And he is black
and I am white, and without meaning or
trying to I must profit from our history,
the way he absorbs the murderous beams of the

nation's heart, as black cotton
absorbs the heat of the sun and holds it. There is
no way to know how easy this
white skin makes my life, this
life he could break so easily, the way I
think his own back is being broken, the
rod of his soul that at birth was dark and
fluid, rich as the heart of a seedling
ready to thrust up into any available light.

DANIEL TOBIN

The Other Half

When the well-to-do were sleeping
in their uptown beds, I prowled
the roosts and hovels of the poor
hauling my cyclops camera
into every flyblown tenement
from Five Points to Chatham Street
to cut my newsman's teeth on portraits
of the other half crowded in bunks,
or huddled alone in tramp's nests,
wretched as the rags hawked from carts.

Dirt and desolation. Darkened wells
where the rent collector's knocks
stammer from cellar to attic room.
Through these firetraps I made
my own midnight rounds, hungry
to shock the privileged from their dream
of gardens and lace, the slumlord
from his pious indignation,
to light the lives of the common horde,
and rested my case with the governor.

I had been there myself, blank face
in a station house hall, staring
from a line-up of vagrants and thugs.

No work for the immigrant, white
as I was, from Copenhagen,
thrown in with the like of Joss and Jew,
Negro, Italian, Teuton, and Paddy.
Three years I traffic'd with boot-blacks,
coal-heavers, my clothes silvered
with the spindrift of ash-bins.

I rose from all that, like a man self-saved,
and made my own indignant descent
to bear witness to the waste,
the upas tree of capital and greed.
These pictures—Street Arabs asleep,
Swamp Angels in their lair, those boys
fetching growlers of beer—bring back
a history, foretell what never ends:
the light ignited at my pistol's crack,
some child's eyes blinding in the flash.

Blackbottom

When relatives came from out of town,
we would drive down to Blackbottom,
drive slowly down the congested main streets
    —Beaubien and Hastings—
trapped in the mesh of Saturday night.
Freshly escaped, black middle class,
we snickered, and were proud;
the louder the streets, the prouder.
We laughed at the bright clothes of a prostitute,
a man sitting on a curb with a bottle in his hand.
We smelled barbecue cooking in dented washtubs,
    and our mouths watered.
As much as we wanted it we couldn't take the chance.

Rhythm and blues came from the windows, the throaty
    voice of a woman lost in the bass, in the drums, in the
    dirty down and out, the grind.
"I love to see a funeral, then I know it ain't mine."
We rolled our windows down so that the waves rolled over us
    like blood.
We hoped to pass invisibly, knowing on Monday we would
    return safely to our jobs, the post office and classroom.
We wanted our sufferings to be offered up as tender meat,
and our triumphs to be belted out in raucous song.

We had lost our voice in the suburbs, in Conant Gardens,
    where each brick house delineated a fence of silence;
we had lost the right to sing in the street and damn creation.

We returned to wash our hands of them,
to smell them
whose very existence
tore us down to the human.

American Hero

I have nothing to lose tonight.
All my men surround me, panting,
as I spin the ball above our heads
on my middle finger.
It's a shimmering club light
and I'm dancing, slick in my sweat.
Squinting, I aim at the hole
fifty feet away. I let the tension go.
Shoot for the net. Choke it.
I never hear the ball
slap the backboard. I slam it
through the net. The crowd goes wild
for our win. I scored
thirty-two points this game
and they love me for it.
Everyone hollering
is a friend tonight.
But there are towns,
certain neighborhoods
where I'd be hard pressed
to hear them cheer
if I move on the block.

black history/white legacy part 1

for the housekeepers of my childhood: Priscilla, Blanche, and Pearl

how do i march in the parade and not be a hypocrite?
how do i raise my fist and feel pride?

it's not just you on a displaced continent
which of course you know better than i
but you know better than i which continent
to miss and mourn for, celebrate and emulate (without reservations)

i have inherited the okra, the biscuits, and the blues, too
we both know my mother learned to make not from her mother
but from her mother's maids—the same maids who raised me
called maids because slaves was no longer right
but anything else would have meant admission
and a significant raise

so their well-kneaded bread kept us fed
and their encouragement kept us reading
their wagged fingers kept us in line
all while the other hand folded our laundry
and dusted our things collected and unused

their cleaning up after us kept us honest
as they always uncovered our secrets
yet always kept them

we fully believed in their omniscient powers
obeyed their heavy gaze and dismayed at their shaking heads
where we merely rolled our eyes at our own mothers'

but they never looked in our eyes when parents were around
which, i guess, is how we knew never to speak to them
in front of grown ups—a silent pact

but alone we drove them crazy distracting their work
as we circled 'round them with our tethered ponies and pool toys
assuming a friendship and always puzzled when they went home—
(*they went home*)

with untouched leftovers and refrigerator boxes—
to their children
(*they had children*)

but their children knew refrigerator boxes make great spaceships
because they were being raised on imagination
while we were being raised on things
and they knew leftovers were better than nothing left

because they wanted more for their children
while we simply always wanted more
because their children went to college
on hard work and a first generation's privilege
while we dropped out of college out of spite

black history/white legacy part 2

but now that i'm grown i want to march in the parade
because i know things still aren't right and the more
true freedom you have, the more we all stand to inherit

how do i march in the parade and not be a hypocrite?
how do i raise my fist and feel pride?

i want to march in the parade
and learn what pride without prejudice looks like
and where it can take us

i want to march in the parade
and say teach me how to write poetry from boxing rings
and come out swinging my anger into activism

i want our senators to march in the parade
and say teach us how to stretch a dollar
and make good on our centuries-old promissory note

i want our parents to march in the parade
saying teach us how to take care of our children and parents
without shipping them off to institutions

i want our boys to march in the parade
and say teach us how to own our own pain
without shooting up school yards and post offices

i want our victims to march in the parade
saying teach us forgiveness
and how to draw strength from our knowing

i want our artists to march in the parade
saying teach us how to see beauty
in curves, the up-beat, and non-neutral colors
(and for the love of god teach our
britney-tiphany-teenie-boppers how to sing)

i want our doctors, scientists & engineers to put down
the plastic surgery scalpels & march in the parade saying
teach us how to explore space from refrigerator box rockets

i want our presidents to march in the parade
saying teach us how to put down our missiles
and move mountains with non-violent marches

i want our preachers and bible-thumpers to march in the parade
saying teach us that neighborhoods are congregations
and porch fronts are temples

i want us all to march in the parade
Till we have the courage to demand our dead
be returned from Money and insist these boxes be broke open . . .

oh, to bound up off that curb & join the parade
without asking you teach us, show us, accommodate us,
do us one more thing

N.O.

'bones older than god and mightier
that had blown blaring,
march parading through your dreams
riffed by a thousand, calloused,
dark blue, delicate fingers
now couldn't play the smallest processional.

as effective as a soggy baguette
clogged with foggy waters
they gurgled with mud
and spewed sludge—
we could not even save
two quarter notes
before the flood.

brown-faced mothers
shouting from the rooftops
for their babies to be saved
their calls were ignored
even our apathy was bored
so room and board
was a sweltering stadium
with ants eating away at the tedium
and mosquitoes thriving on the
anarchaic state of them.

ancient aged and cajun caged
we had always turned our cheek on them
while they quietly, smiledly built our heritage
and wrote our theme songs
played out sugar bread and sea-fed sandwiches
gave birth to those coping hues
electric guitar blues
inspired beatledom
and throaty tom waits for no man.

able to eke out more life in their dying
then we know to do in our living,
all this time they refused
staying afloat on saintly notes
they drowned out the sound of poverty
with the music of 'bones.

but who plays the music
when its a funeral you're burying?
we even killed the respect out of death.

we mistook their humility for humidity.
they did not bow their heads
from heat, but from gratitude
to the many spirits
who walk the street
but up against a wall
like peeling wallpaper
we cannot resist
the temptation to rip them off.

only willing to witness once a year
at party gras and only then to drink
to forget and glamorize the po' boy
though he still did not get rich
the rest of the time
they just went on, and on without us.

damned behind a levy engineered
only to keep them in, not keep them safe,
the great storm of irony and pillage
poured such rain and wind force on their village
they died in the dark long ago.

and then,
only to wash
the bodies out to sea
katrina came
and with her
the crews of t.v.
so we could
finally see.

GUSTAVO PÉREZ FIRMAT

Summer Nights

When our children grow up
in North Carolina
who will they be?
It's not so easy, Rosa,
everything has consequences,
gives you something to think about
on summer nights.
Where's the city, the hub, the conversations?
Why should we trade passion for pastoral
when neither one of us was born on a farm?
It's not so easy, Rosa,
everything has consequences,
gives you something to think about
on summer nights.

Trace

for Amiri Baraka, Derya, and my sister Stephanie

red hot black stones
beneath thick forest green
army blankets
repelling chill and bite
lying outside
deep inside   blue
light cast on and from ice
blanketing ground in sheets
layered   fourteen times
each   sheet one-inch thick
mirroring   seven point
suns so far away
they look like glitter
and remind us of the dual sun era
when rattlesnake brought back
the daughter sun to the Tsa la gi
seeds   implanted
forever   in the snags of
our minds   carefully folded
into clusters   retaining
their impact and our knowledge
hiding out in our home
the place we held onto

when they tore our people
from its cradle and forced
the walk where
more than three thousand died
where some of us hid even then
and brought back
the sacred heart   of our
emergence place through
a sympathetic white man
one we   took in because he
had ears and heard us and cared
where they made even this
privately owned Indian land
a reservation anyway   and forced
more of us to leave again
in political protest of reservations
and those who stayed to live
as they decided,   some
when venturing out into
the lands that by nature
also are ours   now occupied
by the Americans were even
to be humiliated
to have to use the
color-coded bathrooms
they set up for
the Africans who turned around   breaking
bondage, eliminating constraint, more constraints endured by
the Asians who had left the plains rails,

coming here to this piedmont,
the Latinos who labored
still in migrant campos   and the people
The People   who were
at home here always
even in the 1970s
color-coded bathrooms
white/colored   where
even a blonde-headed girl-child
entered into in public
though she could have   evaded
this humiliation   but refused
to go where some relatives
could not go   because
they were darker complexioned
hiding out in secret
perspectives as old as the
sky above and as
warm as the stones lying
now   beneath her feet
cool, crisp, clean   breaths
inhaled in
tenacious reveling
yellow strands entangled,   mixed,
with the black hair her
sister threw over her
back in lying   to rest   beside   her.

Black, Not Hispanic

I lament the lack of Spanish on my tongue
like a pregnant woman's cravings on an August
night when the belly is too big for the car and
hot is alive in every swollen joint.

I remember my Mother changing her mind about my color
when I was ten. I was Black. The next day, I was Hispanic.
She talked of Panama—
a slip of land that looked like my Daddy
colored Grandmothers. I checked the box marked Black

anyway. She couldn't see me. I had not changed since
the time I was four when I was informed firmly about
my Blackness. It made sense back then. The word coffee
has a startling intensity and jolting blood electricity.

My Grandmother tells her life in a rolling sequence
of Intelligentsia identity.
Dates her events along name-calling fashions. In eighty years,
she has been as many flavors of Black as Baskin & Robbins
serves ice cream. South Africa told her

She was White once, when they needed her not to be Black
for eleven days. That story was funny enough for me to want
to stay Black when I was ten. The "in crowd"

served up diversity on the fancy platters of multi-culturalism.
I remember when rainbows

were about God's promise. Instead of a buzz word
stinging like any insect with venom for your veins.
My tongue tangos and salsas. Limbos deftly
under the Queen's English. My Grandmother tongue

was snipped out. Efficient as runaway slave-breaking
techniques. How many languages can they beat out?
How many times will we deny ancestors? Certainly
more than Peter. Rome was an infant dabbling at Empire.

I lament the lack of Spanish on my tongue.
This dance of definitions has become tiring.
I no longer wish to try on names as if
our port of entry was a chic boutique now past its time

and worthy of mourning. One slave name
honors my ancestors. The other maintains an illusion
that we are who colonized us rather
than families of Africans divided by a new world.
These definitions clank and howl.

I hear them like moans bounced off the stench
of ship holds when we fed the Atlantic new salt.

PAT MORA

Legal Alien

Bi-lingual, Bi-cultural,
able to slip from "How's life?"
to *"Me'stan volviendo loca,"*
able to sit in a paneled office
drafting memos in smooth English,
able to order in fluent Spanish
at a Mexican restaurant,
American but hyphenated,
viewed by Anglos as perhaps exotic,
perhaps inferior, definitely different,
viewed by Mexicans as alien,
(their eyes say, "You may speak
Spanish but you're not like me")
an American to Mexicans
a Mexican to Americans
a handy token
sliding back and forth
between the fringes of both worlds
by smiling
by masking the discomfort
of being pre-judged
Bi-laterally.

who am i

wanna be anything but who i am   right proud of my
cherokee roots   a drop of 'kee blood from being
slave raped   massa john traded my right to live freely
for some blankets and beads   ironic trading a slave
to a slave   tribal vote erased my name from rolls

wanna be african, french, irish, german, scotch
a fifty-fifty ratio diluted innumerable times thru a to z
generations   these green eyes tell you i'm not what
i appear so i play my green card whenever i go dancing
dual passports make me black and white

laws tinted my mind and trials made me run from
reality   africa don't want me, france uses me,
ireland spits on me, germany hates me, scotland
laughs at me   america created me and they call me
the absence of color 'cause i've absorbed the light

wanna make my woolly hair straight and straight hair
woolly   bleach the mocha and tan the vanilla
paint brown eyes blue and blue eyes hazel   point my
flat nose and implant whatever ain't growin' accordin'
to my desires

lips plump with love need thinnin' cause love is
not what i'm feeling, while thin lips need filling
to experience what i'm running from   too thin,
too tall, too fat, too small   nippin' and tuckin'
everything that ain't right in my world

filled with hate so long, i don't know how to love what i
was given   trafficking thoughts from outside sources
destroyed my self esteem centuries ago   it's become a
self fulfilling prophecy to wanna be somebody else
channeling cleopatra for beauty tips and Jesus for what to do

artists might have it right painting eyes on elbows and ears
where noses go   smells i see come from someone else's
thoughts   clearly or not, they paint from inside out and
emphasize my distorted perceptions   must my reality be
i don't love the truth of me and the blessing i truly am

The Mulatto to His Critics

Ashamed of my race?
And of what race am I?
I am many in one.
Thru my veins runs the blood
Of Red Man, Black Man, Briton, Celt and Scot,
In warring clash and tumultuous riot.
I welcome all,
But love the blood of the kindly race
That swarthes my skin, crinkles my hair,
And puts sweet music into my soul.

ALICIA CHAMBERS

On the Question of Race

They ask me to write down my race

And I think
And I think
Very seriously

And I consider
Writing down the truth
And have my answer read

I have a strong woman
Colored like coffee
Whispering the secrets of our past
Inside this body

I have a wise man
Dark as chocolate
Beating his drum, fighting for freedom
Inside this body

I have a brave woman
Pale as snow
Reminding that we are more
Than meets the eye
Her secret is safe
Inside this body

I have a lost man
Colored like me
He is weak
Stumbling from place to place
Trying to find his way home
Warning me of everything
I do not want to become

I have all this music inside this body
The rhythms guiding me
Salsa
Meringue
Swing
Songs of freedom and hope
A name that can't begin to
communicate
Where I've been or where I plan to go
Inside this body

They ask me to write down my race

And I think
And I think
Very seriously

And I consider
Writing down the truth
And have my answer read

I have the heart of my great-
grandmother
The strength of mi abuelita
The spirit of my grandfather
And my mother's understanding
Inside this body

I have jacks
Dr. Seuss
Lullaby and Good-night
And marbles
Inside this body

I have Ray Charles
James Taylor
Bob Marley
Sly and the Family Stone
And We Five
Inside this body

I have a brother whose appearance
Does not reveal his culture

I have all our past
And so much future
Inside this body

But I stop and simply write down
"Other"

AURORA LEVINS MORALES

Child of the Americas

I am a child of the Americas,
a light-skinned mestiza of the Caribbean,
a child of many diaspora, born into this continent at a crossroads.

I'm a U.S. Puerto Rican Jew,
a product of the ghettos of New York I have never known.
An immigrant and the daughter and granddaughter of immigrants.
I speak English with passion: It's the tool of my consciousness,
a flashing knife blade of crystal, my tool, my craft.

I am a Caribeña, island grown, Spanish is in my flesh,
ripples from my tongue, lodges in my hips:
the language of garlic and mangoes,
the singing in my poetry, the flying gestures of my hands.
I am of Latinoamérica, rooted in the history of my continent:
I speak from that body.

I am not african. Africa is in me, but I cannot return.
I am not taína. Taíno is in me, but there is no way back.
I am not european. Europe lives in me, but I have no home there.

I am new. History made me. My first language was spanglish.
I was born at the crossroads
and I am whole.

This Face

Eyes like magpies in milk,
the caves of the nose, lips,
the darker petals of pink roses;
it is a face of an Asian
derived from the Malays, the hunters in Java, the
    ancient Chinese
cooling themselves on the banks of the Yangtze,
it is my father's face.

Asian men; in America it could be
another word for mule,
the sterile,
almost female,
the *gook, nips,* and *flips*
who cook beautiful meals with bean sprouts,
cashews, and water chestnuts;
who slice their meats in slivers;
who eat food with sticks like slender fingers;
who do laundry for a living;
who are passive;
who are more cerebral than sexual,
who are prisoners of their genetics:
the undersized, soft frame, bodies almost hairless,
the features of the Mongoloid.

I see the face that looks back at me:
the porcupined eyebrows,
the furrows of the forehead,
the overbite. Same as when I hunch
over a basin of water,
as when I close my eyes to sleep—
it is the face of someone
who favors potatoes;
who has had many affairs with women;
who is the source of my conceit, my Asianness,
my maleness. It is my father's
and I love it.

ALLISON JOSEPH

On Being Told I Don't Speak
Like a Black Person

Emphasize the "h," you ignorant ass,
was what my mother was told
when colonial-minded teachers
slapped her open palm with a ruler
in that Jamaican schoolroom.
Trained in England, they tried
to force their pupils to speak
like Eliza Doolittle after
her transformation, fancying themselves
British as Henry Higgins,
despite dark, sun-ripened skin.
Mother never lost her accent,
though, the music of her voice
charming everyone, an infectious lilt
I can imitate, not duplicate.
No one in the States told her
to eliminate the accent,
my high school friends adoring
the way her voice would lift
when she called me to the phone:
A-lli-son, it's friend Cathy.
Why don't you sound like her?,
they'd ask. I didn't sound

like anyone or anything,
no grating New Yorker nasality,
no fastidious British mannerisms
like the ones my father affected
when he wanted to sell someone
something. And I didn't sound
like a Black American,
college acquaintances observed,
sure they knew what a black person
was supposed to sound like.
Was I supposed to sound lazy,
dropping syllables here, there,
not finishing words but
slurring final letters so that
each sentence joined the next,
sliding past the listener?
Were certain words off limits,
too erudite, too scholarly
for someone with a natural tan?
I asked what they meant,
and they stuttered, blushed,
said *you know, Black English,*
applying what they'd learned
from that semester's text.
Does everyone in your family
speak alike? I'd question,
and they'd say *don't take this*
the wrong way, nothing personal.
Now I realize there's nothing

more personal than speech,
that I don't have to defend
how I speak, how any person,
black, white, chooses to speak.
Let us speak. Let us talk
with the sounds of our mothers
and fathers still reverberating
in our minds, wherever our mothers
or fathers come from:
Arkansas, Belize, Alabama,
Brazil, Aruba, Arizona.
Let us simply speak
to one another,
listen and prize the inflections,
differences, never assuming
how any person will sound
until her mouth opens,
until his mouth opens,
greetings familiar
in any language.

Rice

In our Armenian, Jewish, Negro
mixed-race neighborhood
at five years old
before writing with pencil
when Dr. Seuss was El Rey
I was taught how to cook
the two-times-a-day dish
affectionately known as
"Is There More Rice?"

I stood on a chair
in front of the sink
with mama's Tagalog
mi abuelo's Castilian—
bigas y arroth and
papa's "No butter,
no sugar is good."
I washed the rice three times—

hinogasang ko ang bigas.
I washed the rice twice

El Rey (Spanish)—the king
mi abuelo (Spanish)—my grandfather
hinogasang ko ang bigas (Tagalog)—I washed the rice

in a scarred metal pot
that put stories of slavery and wars
in their mouths.
I washed the rice once—
milky starch disappeared
and the water was clear
enough for their eyes.

I measured the water
according to digits
of my middle finger
this was better than cups
and easier to use.

Mi abuelo would transfer
the pot to the fire—
I napped to Naciemento for cuarenta minutos
while sambas boiled
and lowered the flame,
and when I woke up
arroth-bigas-rice-lutong-kanin
with fish heads and squid
was ready to eat.

They'd tell me that I
was a wonderful cook

cuarenta minutos (Spanish)—forty minutes
lutong kanin (Tagalog)—cooked rice

while I ate with my fingers
instead of a fork
and thought about cooking
the next evening's meal . . .
I decided on seaweed,
Uncle Chico's red snapper,
arroth-bigas-rice, beans
"More rice."
"Sí, there's rice."

MARTA I. VALENTÍN

La Salsa Is Still Very Much Alive in Me

its rhythms grab at my skirt
like cold, hungry men in the pen
the first time they see a woman
after seeing men's asses for much too long
    and she sways, teases the air thick with pride
(pregnant in the night)
the cowbells ringing their upbeat, groove, fink chimes
    La Salsa she comes swiftly through
shoulder to shoulder rumbling
with the bodies of heat
    La Salsa heat
the piano begins to tinkle
and the wrinkles of time fade away
behind the bongo bull
and the trumpet comes searing through
proclaiming loudly:
    La Salsa is here, and she is alive
    For the dead . . . would not remember . . . such pleasures.

The Truth Is

In my left pocket a Chickasaw hand
rests on the bone of the pelvis.
In my right pocket
a white hand. Don't worry. It's mine
and not some thief's.
It belongs to a woman who sleeps in a twin bed
even though she falls in love too easily,
and walks along with hands
in her own empty pockets
even though she has put them in others
for love not money.

About the hands, I'd like to say
I am a tree, grafted branches
bearing two kinds of fruit,
apricots maybe and pit cherries.
It's not that way. The truth is
we are crowded together
and knock against each other at night.
We want amnesty.

Linda, girl, I keep telling you
this is nonsense
about who loved who
and who killed who.

Here I am, taped together
like some old civilian conservation corps
passed by from the great depression
and my pockets are empty.
It's just as well since they are masks
for the soul, and since coins and keys
both have the sharp teeth of property.

Girl, I say,
it is dangerous to be a woman of two countries.
You've got your hands in the dark
of two empty pockets. Even though
you walk and whistle like you aren't afraid
you know which pocket the enemy lives in
and you remember how to fight
so you better keep right on walking.
And you remember who killed who.
For this you want amnesty
and there's that knocking on the door
in the middle of the night.

Relax, there are other things to think about.
Shoes for instance.
Now those are the true masks of the soul.
The left shoe
and the right one with its white foot.

Soul Food

For Cecil

We prepare
the meal together.
I complain,
hurt, reduced to fury
again by their
subtle insults
insinuations
because I am married to you.
Impossible autonomy, no mind
of my own.

You like your fish
crisp, coated with cornmeal,
fried deep,
sliced mangos to sweeten
the tang of lemons.
My fish is raw,
on shredded lettuce,
lemon slices thin as skin,
wasabe burning like green fire.
You bake the cornbread flat
and dip it in

the thick soup
I've brewed from
turkey carcass, rice gruel,
sesame oil and chervil.

We laugh over watermelon
and bubbling cobbler.

You say,
there are few men
who can stand
to have a woman equal,
upright.

This meal,
unsurpassed.

LYN LEVY

Wearing Glasses

once,
    after a meeting
you left your
glasses
    behind the couch
and had to
    come back later
to get them.

and from there
    we began to converse
on the universal hassles of
glasses wearing and
    progressed slowly

into a discussion
on what Blacks and Puerto Ricans
had in common

    and i let you read
    some of my poems
    while we listened to
    Roberta Flack

and our relationship gently
    grew from
    Puerto Ricans in

general
     and Black folks largely
to one Puerto Rican
specifically
     and one Blackwoman
exclusively.

minus talk of the
nation, the Black Panthers
and the Young Lords

and we moved silently on
from Nikki Giovanni and Hernandez Cruz
while constantly warning
each other
     that we must remain uninvolved
uncommitted and objective about
     this whole thing

we barely noticed the difference
except that
     when we were apart
things looked a little
     more dismal and
a little harder to take

while discussing Pitt Street
     and junkies
and Willis Street and
     alcoholics,

we moved slowly to
examine the similar
similar
        styles of Black and Puerto Rican
poets and

        we easily progressed
        toward similar tastes
        in poems and books

and the wine you drank
        i almost liked
we were unconsciously
moved into the realm
of lovers.

when we ultimately discovered
to our amazement
'that something is happening
to us lyn . . .'
        you left for Puerto Rico
where you
        were convicted of
being a revolutionary.

i wish you
        had left
your glasses behind
the couch.

KIMBERLY M. BLAESER

Certificate of Live Birth

I
Shuffling papers
    rushing to find some critical
    form or letter or journal
    mired amid the stacks that have collected
    that I've hidden in every corner of the room

Tiny newborn footprints step out of flatland
    a xerox copy of my birth certificate
Nostalgia
    no time—
Yet as I hold the single sheet
    it shapes itself and curves out of my hand

Chubby ankle circled firmly
    protesting kicking held still
    foot inked
    the page indelibly marked
    with my unwilling signature
Perhaps some memory of that first helplessness
    makes me struggle still against capture
    against hint of bonds—
You won't imprint me again

II
Or perhaps it was your capture
    that so enraged my yet unconscious mind
    that brought me kicking into the world
For yours was the more torturous:
    Father, caucasian.
    Mother, caucasian.
What pain what shame what fear
    must have forced that check in that flatland box?

Mother, should I correct it?

But no it is more accurate
    just as it stands
In that mark I read your life
I read the history of Indian people in this country
It is my heritage more truly than any account of bloodlines
It tells the story of a people's capture
It tells the story of a people's struggle to survive

And, Mother, this poem is the certificate of our live birth
For together we have escaped their capture
Our time together outdistances their prison

It stands in ruins within the circle of our lives:
    Father, caucasian.
    Mother, American Indian.
    Daughter, mixedblood.

C. K. WILLIAMS

Racists

Vas en Afrique! Back to Africa! the butcher we used to patronize
    in the Rue Cadet market,
beside himself, shrieked at a black man in an argument the rest
    of the import of which I missed
but that made me anyway for three years walk an extra street to
    a shop of definitely lower quality
until I convinced myself that probably I'd misunderstood that
    other thing and could come back.
Today another black man stopped, asking something that again
    I didn't catch, and the butcher,
who at the moment was unloading his rotisserie, slipping the
    chickens off their heavy spit,
as he answered—how get this right?—casually but accurately
    brandished the still-hot metal,
so the other, whatever he was there for, had subtly to lean away
    a little, so as not to flinch.

KIMBERLY DIXON

Close Quarters

When
her hand
brushes
my shoulder
I feel her
bones, and her
mother's bones
when she slapped
my mother, or
maybe not
our mothers
but somewhere
in there some
one of hers
slapped some
one of mine
so I
bristle,
but get another
touch, as if
to sandpaper,
prick, while
beads of
red memory

well, her
white claws
drag me
across
a minefield.

Sammy Davis, Jr.

who can make the sun rise?
sprinkle it with dew . . .

she awakened me with tears
get up baby / get up & pack
martin luther king, jr. has been shot & killed
you & i baby / we're goin to
atlanta

mom & i flew there to pay
our respects
say goodbye to a man & hello
to his dream
i have a dream
that one day . . .
we crashed a hotel segregated
high rise tower on peachtree street
with white valets
& nervous executives
eager to appease they sorta
welcomed our presence kinda
treated us proper like
tellin us 'bout all the amenities this four star
had to offer

so many things but i only heard
the pool / the pool
we have such a lovely pool

so first things first
i went to swim
lap after lap
back 'n' forth
like esther mae williams come down outta da hood
oblivious
to the scavengers & piranha
angry white men pointin / disgusted
flustered white women in high heels / appalled
there's a NEGRO in our pool
a COLORED girl, i tell you
mommy, will she hurt the water
we can't go in til she comes out

i executed my backstroke
eyes climbin high towards heaven
& fixed upon hip black man stridin balcony tough
jumpin / projectin
non-containin himself
you stay in that water, girl
you swim & swim some more
doncha pay no mind to those circling sharks
look up/ see god / & swim girl swim

sammy took us out to lunch
said what i had done was no different
than martin or rosa or harriet even

cuz that is how we swim this meet
just livin life as we choose to live
one backstroke at a time

TOI DERRICOTTE

The Struggle

We didn't want to be white—or did we?
What did we want?
In two bedrooms, side by side,
four adults, two children.
My aunt and uncle left before light.
My father went to the factory, then the cleaners.
My mother vacuumed, ironed, cooked,
pasted war coupons. In the afternoon
she typed stencils at the metal kitchen table.
I crawled under pulling on her skirt.
What did we want?
As the furniture became modern, the carpet deep, the white
ballerina on the mantel lifted her arms like some girl near
        terror;
the Degas ballerinas bowed softly in a group, a gray sensual
        beauty.
What did we push ourselves out of ourselves
to do? Our hands
on the doors, cooking utensils, keys; our hands
folding the paper money, tearing the bills.

In the Elementary School Choir

I had never seen a cornfield in my life,
I had never been to Oklahoma,
But I was singing as loud as anyone,
"Oh what a beautiful morning. . . . The corn
Is as high as an elephant's eye,"
Though I knew something about elephants I thought,
Coming from the same continent as they did,
And they being more like camels than anything else.

And when we sang from *Meet Me in St. Louis,*
"Clang, clang, clang went the trolley,"
I remembered the ride from Ramleh Station
In the heart of Alexandria
All the way to Roushdy where my grandmother lived,
The autos on the roadway vying
With mule carts and bicycles,
The Mediterranean half a mile off on the left,
The air smelling sharply of diesel and salt.

It was a problem which had dogged me
For a few years, this confusion of places,
And when in 5th grade geography I had pronounced
"Des Moines" as though it were a village in France,
Mr. Kephart led me to the map on the front wall,
And so I'd know where I was,

Pressed my forehead squarely against Iowa.
Des Moines, he'd said. Rhymes with coins.

Now we were singing "zippidy-doo-dah, zippidy-ay,"
And every song we'd sung had in it
Either sun or bluebirds, fair weather
Or fancy fringe, O beautiful America!
And one tier below me,
There was Linda Deemer with her amber waves
And lovely fruited plains,
And she was part of America too
Along with sun and spacious sky
Though untouchable, and as distant
As purple mountains of majesty.

"This is my country," we sang,
And a few years ago there would have been
A scent of figs in the air, mangoes,
And someone playing the oud along a clear stream.

But now it was "My country 'tis of thee"
And I sang it out with all my heart
And now with Linda Deemer in mind.
"Land where my fathers died," I bellowed,
And it was not too hard to imagine
A host of my great-uncles and -grandfathers
Stunned from their graves in the Turkish interior
And finding themselves suddenly
On a rock among maize and poultry
And Squanto shaking their hands.

How could anyone not think America
Was exotic when it had Massachusetts
And the long tables of thanksgiving?
And how could it not be home
If it were the place where love first struck?

We had finished singing.
The sun was shining through large windows
On the beatified faces of all
Who had sung well and with feeling.
We were ready to file out and march back
To our room where Mr. Kephart was waiting.
Already Linda Deemer had disappeared
Into the high society of the hallway.
One day I was going to tell her something.
Des Moines, I was saying to myself,
Baton Rouge. Terre Haute. Boise.

In Between

I always keep a white man on my left and a
black man on my right.
I always stand in between holding hands.

Sometimes I walk with one and come back
later for the other.
Sometimes I don't see either
for a long time.
Because I change my ways and both are
suddenly black,
or magically white.

I lose touch when they're both the same.
I don't know which is bad and
which is good.
What does it really matter,
when I'm violet in between?

Black, White and Red

Mama says
I got black in my blood
So I cut my thumb
I only saw red

Well, maybe it's
Somewhere else
So I cut my toe
Red there too

Maybe around my heart
That's where they say
All the blood goes
Nope, red again

I cut my thumb
Toe and heart
Don't see black blood
Just red, red, red

When I told someone
What I found
They said to me
Boy are you dumb

Black blood ain't black
It's red
Just like white blood ain't white
It's red too

Well, if black blood is red
And white blood is red
How in the world
Can we be so confused

CHARLES H. JOHNSON

Colored People

When I was growing up
on Folsom Street in West Philadelphia
everyone was colorless
but the world insisted on calling us colored.
There was Mr. Ray the candy store owner
on the corner down the block
selling happiness in pretzel sticks
two for a penny, or peppermint balls
so chilly hard they made your ears pop
if you tried to crack them with your teeth.
Mr. Johnson the grocer across the street
with an open-door policy on an ice cream freezer
that held the creamiest fudgecicles
available one a day for just the right "please"
and somehow got paid for by the end of the week.
Mr. Joyner the dry cleaner around the corner
worked miracles behind a big window
shielded by a dark green plastic
protecting his labor from the sunlight
while concealing his steamy alchemy.
Mr. Moffitt the shoe repairman next door
down a magical flight of stairs
into a basement smelling of leather and glue
echoing with the hammering of a self-made man
who just for the asking would nail

silvery metal taps to your shoes
so you could stomp down the street
to whatever beat you made up.
Everyone was colorful in those days—
Clydie my best friend, Butch Baker the bully,
Patsy who showed me how to work bubble gum
just right until I could splatter
a pink sphere all over my face.
Only the memories are colored;
not the people because they were real.

my dream about being white

hey music and
me
only white,
hair a flutter of
fall leaves
circling my perfect
line of a nose,
no lips,
no behind, hey
white me
and i'm wearing
white history
but there's no future
in those clothes
so i take them off and
wake up
dancing.

black roots

a mocha-colored
silver-rooted
woman with con-
ditioned flat-
ironed hair

said to me with my
spiral-rodded do
"the only people
wearing curls
these days
are niggers"

unable to see
that we interweave
strands by threes to
honor ancestors
as sable as she

and

we kinky curl
twirl and twist
to blend bland
rules on jobs

in which we dread-
lock-minded airs
of culture shock
as we all muddle thru
this "melting pot"

because she
just like back
in the day
still chooses
to play it
straight.

mixed use

dedicated to Sheila Broderick

they used girls like me
instead of mannequins
in the glass windows
of the Limited Too
at the Fashion Mall
in Plantation, Florida
on weekends

underweight girls like me
they found us
slightly
more alive
than plastic

i imagine that sometimes
your weekdays are like
my saturdays were then
a public stillness
breathing disguised as nothing
a mandate (not) to make eye contact
a fear of
a hunger for
the laughter that could make it
all fall apart

they used girls like me
instead of iron
as anchors
on the Paideia High School track team
4 by 4 relay squad
all over Georgia

conveniently black girls like me
they called us
natural talent

i imagine that sometimes
your weekdays are like
my saturdays were then
a chronic inability to stay
between the lines
a dizzy aversion
to running in circles
a tight urge
to steal the baton
and run towards where home might be
forgetting the girls that depend on you

i have no way of knowing
what any day
any week of yours has been
but i want to know
how do you feel

useful?

un/exceptional vernacular

her skin is parallel to night
hair as kinky as good sex
and her thickness bars
her from gracing the covers
of colorful magazines
that promote skin deep beauty
in only high and yellow tones

she can't jump double dutch
or french braid and ain't
had no chittlins
but her negro-tude
can still whip up
real soul food
to dish out to folk

who say she
ain't black 'cause she
don't tawk lak dis
or ack lak dat
and likewise to folk
who say she isn't
black because she
talks like this
instead of like that

but it's only proper
for her to serve what
her soul really has to
offer to folk who label
her type as exceptional
and to folk who label
her type as oreos
instead of pretentiously
feeding into their
stereotypes by asking

just what the
kcuf does she lack
that they and dem
call black??

Blonde White Women

They choke cities like snowstorms.

On the morning train, I flip through my *Ebony*,
marveling at the bargain basement prices
for reams of straightened hair
and bleaches for the skin. Next to me,
skinny pink fingers rest upon a briefcase,
shiver a bit under my scrutiny.
Leaving the tunnel, we hurtle into hurting sun.
An icy brush paints the buildings
with shine, fat spirals of snow
become blankets, and Boston stops breathing.

It is my habit to count them. So I search
the damp, chilled length of the train car
and look for their candle flames of hair,
the circles of blood at their cheeks,
that curt dismissing glare
reserved for the common, the wrinkled, the black.

I remember striving for that breathlessness,
toddling my five-year-old black butt around
with a dull gray mophead covering my
nappy hair, wishing myself golden.
Pressing down hard with my

carnation pink Crayola, I filled faces
in coloring books, rubbed the waxy stick
across the back of my hand until the skin broke.

When my mop hair became an annoyance
to my mother, who always seemed to be mopping,
I hid beneath my father's white shirt,
the sleeves hanging down on either side of my head,
the coolest white light pigtails.
I practiced kissing, because to be blonde and white
meant to be kissed, and my fat lips slimmed
around words like "delightful" and "darling."
I hurt myself with my own beauty.

When I was white, my name was Donna.
My teeth were perfect; I was always out of breath.

In first grade, my blonde teacher
hugged me to her because I was the first
in my class to read, and I thought the rush
would kill me. I wanted her to swallow
me, to be my mother, to be the first fire
moving in my breast. But when she pried
me away, her cool blue eyes shining with
righteousness and too much touch,
I saw how much she wanted to wash.

She was not my mother,
the singing Alabama woman
who shook me to sleep

and fed me from her fingers.
I could not have been blacker
than I was at that moment.
My name is Patricia Ann.

Even crayons fail me now—
I can find no color darker,
more beautiful, than I am.
This train car grows tense with me.
I pulse, steady my eyes,
shake the snow from my short black hair,
and suddenly I am surrounded by snarling madonnas
demanding that I explain
my treachery.

NORA NARANJO-MORSE

The Living Exhibit Under the Museum's Portal

Arriving with high hopes on a breezy March day
    to sell these forms I've made from clay.
    My pocketbook empty, as I lay my blanket down.
We arrive from all directions:
    Cochiti,
        Zuni,
            The Navajo
                and Pueblos.
Selling our blankets,
    bread
        and beads.
We bargain back and forth with tourists,
    and among ourselves . . .
    we must love to bargain.
My friend from Zuni tells me business is slow,
    as she keeps her hands busy, rearranging
    necklaces in single file, on black polyester.
    "Damn," she says, "to think, I could be sitting
    in a warm office right this minute, drinking
    hot chocolate and typing business letters
    for some honky."
A tourist and potential customer blurts out:
    "Excuse me, but do any of you Indians speak English?"
    I answer too politely, hating myself for doing so,

thinking it must be my empty pocketbook
talking for me.
The Indian tribes represented, line quietly against the stark,
white museum wall, as each new day introduces
throngs of tourists, filing past our blankets
fixed in orderly fashion upon red bricks.
Visitors looking for mementos to take home,
that will remind them of the curiously
silent Indians, wrapped tightly in colorful
shawls, just like in the postcards.
Huddling together for warmth, we laugh, remembering
that sexy redhead last summer, who
bent down to pick up a necklace and
ripped her tight white pants.
Casually interested, we watch as Delbert, a city Indian,
hiding behind mirrored sunglasses,
pulls up at noon, to lay his blanket down.
He's come to sell brass and silver
earcuffs he and his girlfriend made.
Delbert sets up, while in the truck
his girlfriend sleeps off last night's party.
My friend is right, business is slow as the late afternoon breeze
hurries customers away from our blankets,
toward the Indian art galleries,
leaving us to feel the sting of cold
through layers of our woolen protection.
The sun fades into the Southwestern corner of the plaza
casting large, cold shadows that signal
the end of our day together.

Quietly we pack for home, bundling our wares
carefully in baskets and old grocery crates.
Back to:
    Cochiti,
       Zuni,
          The Navaho
           and Pueblos.
Tomorrow we will arrive, again with high hopes,
    empty pocketbooks
       and our friendships right in place.

PETER BLUE CLOUD

The Old Man's Lazy,

I heard the Indian Agent say,
has no pride, no get up
and go. Well, he came out
here and walked around my
place, that agent. Steps
all thru the milkweed and
curing wormwood; tells me
my place is overgrown
and should be made use
of.

The old split cedar
fence stands at many
angles, and much of it
lies on the ground like
a curving sentence of
stick writing. An old
language, too, black with
age, with different
shades of green of moss
and lichen.
         He always
says he understands us
Indians,
         and why don't

I fix the fence at least;
so I took some fine
hawk feathers fixed
to a miniature woven
shield
        and hung this
from an upright post
near the house.
                              He
came by last week
and looked all around
again, eyed the feathers
for a long time.
                        He didn't
say anything, and he didn't
smile even, or look within
himself for the hawk.

Maybe sometime I'll
tell him that the fence
isn't mine to begin with,
but was put up by
the white guy who used
to live next door.
                          It was
years ago. He built a cabin,
then put up the fence. He
only looked at me once,
after his fence was up,

he nodded at me as if
to show that he knew I
was here, I guess.

     It was
a pretty fence, enclosing
that guy, and I felt lucky
to be on the outside
of it.

 Well, that guy
dug holes all over his
place, looking for gold,
and I guess

     he never
found any. I watched
him grow old for over
twenty years, and bitter,
I could feel his anger
all over the place.

     And
that's when I took to
leaving my place to do
a lot of visiting.

     Then
one time I came home
and knew he was gone
for good.

My children would
always ask me why I

didn't move to town
and be closer to them.

Now, they
tell me I'm lucky to be
living way out here.
                    And
they bring their children
and come out and visit me,
and I can feel that they
want to live out here
too, but can't
for some reason, do it.

Each day
a different story is
told me by the fence,
the rain and wind and snow,
the sun and moon shadows,
this wonderful earth,
        this Creation.
I tell my grandchildren
many of these stories,
        perhaps
this too is one of them.

Doreen

Doreen had a round face.
She tried to change it.
Everybody made fun
of her in school.

Her eyes so narrow
they asked if she could see,
called her Moonface and
Slits.

Doreen frost tipped her hair,
ratted it five inches high,
painted her eyes round,
glittering blue shadow up to her brow.

Made her look sad
even when she smiled.

She cut gym all the time
because the white powder on her neck
and face would streak
when she sweat.

But Doreen had boobs
more than most of us Japanese girls
so she wore tight sweaters

and low cut dresses
even in winter.

She didn't hang
with us,
since she put so much time
into changing her face.

White boys
would snicker when she passed by
and word got around
that Doreen
went all the way,
smoked and drank beer.

She told us
she met a veteran
fresh back from Korea.

Fresh back
his leg
still puckered pink
from landmines.

She told us
it was a kick
to listen to his stories
about how they'd torture
the gooks
hang them from trees

by their feet
grenades
in their crotch
and watch
them sweat.

I asked her
why she didn't dig brothers.

And her eyes
would disappear
laughing
so loud
she couldn't hear herself.

One day,
Doreen riding fast
with her friend
went through the windshield
and tore off
her skin
from scalp to chin.

And we were sad.

Because
no one could remember
Doreen's face.

SUSAN CLEMENTS

Matinee

Two o'clock on a Saturday afternoon in November,
your father drops you off near the worn steps
of the Manor movie house, the marquee
blinking in a relay of hot lights and foot-high
letters you are too young to read. You clutch
your silver quarter tight in your small hand
as your father reaches past you and pushes open
the car door, nudges you out with his smile
to where other children crowd up to the box
office, screaming and yelling in their bright coats.
You remember the phrase "Let's pretend" that the new
girl on your street taught you through the summer,
always wanting you to play hateful "house," to pretend
tameness when your own blood ran wild with foxes
and invisible deer. Still, you fell in love with the word—
pretend, now, you are a Sleeping Beauty glittering
your way through an ancient war of rough bodies until
you reach the theater's magical cave, hunch down
in a torn seat in the first row, lifting your face
to the safety of the blank screen. You drift among smells
of hot balls, jujubes and cherry dots, hotness and sweetness
on a hundred tongues, savor salty popcorn from a cardboard
carnival box. In the musty shadows the screen swells with
Hollywood technicolor, cowboys-and-Indians, Indians swooping

down on painted ponies, scalping innocent whites, raising
even your hair as you sit, petrified, by war whoops
and swirling hatchet blades, and brown faces webbed
with black. Like the other children, you cheer,
throw popcorn when the good cowboys kill every Indian
at movie's end, and the hero in his white hat points out,
"The only good Indian is a dead one." You stumble
outdoors, wedged in the crowd. A dark-eyed boy pulls
your long hair, and just as you get ready to kill him
you spot your father waiting for you in his old car.
You climb in and tell him how horrible Indians are.
He listens as the first snow of the year starts to fall,
turns on the windshield wipers as you both yield in silence
to their measured slaps, ice crystals melting inward
on the window glass. Christmas bulbs strung along bare wires
over Main Street shimmer, blue green red, in the snow dusk.
"Your grandfather was Indian," your father says at last.
"You're part Indian. Indians were here first, like the first snow."
You cross your arms as he backs out into a cloud of smoke.
The snow drops into the lights of town like feathers from a vast
and wounded bird. Pretend, *pretend*. You glitter as you fall.

Election Time

Names will change
faces will change
but not much else
the President will still be white
and male
and wasp
still speak with forked tongue
still wear red, white and blue underwear
still sleep on white sheets
in a white house
still surround himself with white men
still believe that white is the best thing to be
still read all white newspapers
that only talk about Blacks in connection with crime
still fly in white Air Force One
still worship a white Jesus
still pray to a white God
still go on vacation
where white people lie on white sand beaches
still white out his mistakes
still issue white papers
still throw out little white balls
on opening day
still uphold the laws of dead white men

still dream about big white monuments
and big white memorials
ain't nothin' changed
ain't nothin' changed at all

The Change

The season turned like the page of a glossy fashion magazine.
In the park the daffodils came up
and in the parking lot, the new car models were on parade.

Sometimes I think that nothing really changes—

The young girls show the latest crop of tummies,
    and the new president proves that he's a dummy.

But remember the tennis match we watched that year?
Right before our eyes

some tough little European blonde
pitted against that big black girl from Alabama,
cornrowed hair and Zulu bangles on her arms,
some outrageous name like Vondella Aphrodite—

We were just walking past the lounge
    and got sucked in by the screen above the bar,
and pretty soon
we started to care about who won,

putting ourselves into each whacked return
as the volleys went back and forth and back
like some contest between
the old world and the new,

and you loved her complicated hair
and her to-hell-with-everybody stare,
and I,
        I couldn't help wanting
the white girl to come out on top,
because she was one of my kind, my tribe,
with her pale eyes and thin lips

and because the black girl was so big
and so black,
                so unintimidated,

hitting the ball like she was driving the Emancipation
        Proclamation
down Abraham Lincoln's throat,
like she wasn't asking anyone's permission.

There are moments when history
passes you so close
                you can smell its breath,
you can reach your hand out
                        and touch it on its flank,

and I don't watch all that much *Masterpiece Theatre*,
but I could feel the end of an era there

in front of those bleachers full of people
in their Sunday tennis-watching clothes

as that black girl wore down her opponent
then kicked her ass good
then thumped her once more for good measure

and stood up on the red clay court
holding her racket over her head like a guitar.

And the little pink judge
                          had to climb up on a box
to put the ribbon on her neck,
still managing to smile into the camera flash,
even though everything was changing

and in fact, everything had already changed—

Poof, remember? It was the twentieth century almost gone,
we were there,

and when we went to put it back where it belonged,
it was past us
and we were changed.

The Search

I
When I was whipped
for playing with blacks,
cold shivered my spine.

When my pastor wouldn't let
blacks attend church,
my bones turned brittle.

Cold crept through my soles,
froze my feet in place
when whites tortured black friends.

At eighteen, I fled twisted roots,
escaped cold racial prejudice,
spent forty years gasping for breath,

Until one night on DC streets,
when the White House bunkered down
behind barricades, guards, phone taps,

I visited our historic monuments,
cold imprisoned tigers
of a broken nation.

I heard an old fashioned bell ring
in a human church steeple.
It beckoned me to enter.

Alone in a handicap pew,
I bowed my head to prayer
by a black female minister.

Faces from where I fled
appeared on moonbeams
through altar windows.

The congregation sang
I Feel Good,
Celebrating Souls' Godfather.

I listened to *Spirit of Life.*
Tears soaked my shirt.
I yearned this song a lifetime.

I inhaled its warmth,
my heart sprung alive
as blacks, gays, whites embraced.

The following Sundays I returned
with tissue, listened to sermons
about living without prejudice

until July 27th, 2008, a man enters
a Knoxville church, his heart frozen
like mine used to be.

He murders two, wounds seven,
members from all faiths,
all races, sexual orientations.

II
My daughter's mother asserts
Unitarian is not a real church,
not a bible church

where my little white girl
had a black heart because she asked,
"Why doesn't God love everyone?"

Frightened, she ran crying,
crossed three six lane streets,
rushing from fear to be punished.

Reminds me to remember decades searching
for love, to remember lives sacrificed
for social justice.

My minister's voice rattles, shouts,
"Last stop, life's crossroads."
We sing *Spirit of Life*,

and I will keep singing,
and singing,
and singing.

Seeing Armstrong: 1931

Charlie Black   was a white boy
    It was 1931
The town was Austin Texas
    Louis Armstrong   played a horn

The venue   was the Driskill
    Black entered
              through the front door
He played   *with his eyes closed*
   things that had never
             existed before

Charlie Black   a white boy
   saw a black man
          play a horn
He was the first
       genius
        I had seen

It was 1931
      it was Texas
         Black
was white   Black was
        sixteen when he went
   to the Driskill that night

For a Southern   white boy
      can you understand
                              what it meant
      to see genius for the
                        first time in a
                                    black man?

                    *

Linda Brown was a black girl
      in Kansas
              in '54
John Brown had left the state
                        bleeding Kansas

      a century before

Charles Black
                    was now   a lawyer
      on Thurgood Marshall's team
Linda Brown
                    was a black girl
      Her parents had a

Linda Brown
                    was Homer Plessy
      her school
                        his railway car
Linda Brown was   Dred Scott
      starting
                  the same war

                    129

Charlie   Black was a white boy
      in 1931
The road before him led
      from Austin
                        to beyond

That's when I started walking
      to the Brown
                        case where I belonged
The venue   was the Driskill
      Louis Armstrong   sang a song

Frederick Douglass

When it is finally ours, this freedom, this liberty, this beautiful
and terrible thing, needful to man as air,
usable as earth; when it belongs at last to all,
when it is truly instinct, brain matter, diastole, systole,
reflex action; when it is finally won; when it is more
than the gaudy mumbo jumbo of politicians:
this man, this Douglass, this former slave, this Negro
beaten to his knees, exiled, visioning a world
where none is lonely, none hunted, alien,
this man, superb in love and logic, this man
shall be remembered. Oh, not with statues' rhetoric,
not with legends and poems and wreaths of bronze alone,
but with the lives grown out of his life, the lives
fleshing his dream of the beautiful, needful thing.

PAULA COLE JONES

On the Wings of a Bird

A modern day warrior
A man of his word
Rose towards the sun
On the wings of a bird

His face etched in ebony
Armor of gold
The depths of the sea
Could embody his soul

The ancestral spirits
Endowed him with sight
The cries of his people
Prepared him to fight

His foes cast out nets
And with lies dimmed the lights
But the undaunted hero
Rose to new heights

Over rain thirsty rivers
And forests ablaze
Over greed and abandon
And human malaise

He planted his sword
Down deep in the boughs
He silenced the tremors
And true to his vows

He rose like the phoenix
His power conferred
His face towards the sun
On the wings of a bird

WENDY ROSE

Naayawva Taawi

Left in the field
among big-bellied ewes
tightly rusted stuff of borders,
bales of fence wire
sit in the wind
solid
as if on full bellies

and it was not
the garbage you thought
nor discarded nor useless
but look   the small birds
with speckled wings and black heads
have made their nests there
with barley chaff and string,
bits of alfalfa,
singing as sweetly in the wire
as in the willow.

In the wind
of sage, sweetgrass,
you called us

Naayawva Taawi (Hopi)—Fight Song

          guteater and squaw
          savage and drunk
we who finished in the field
the job you began,
we who honored your fine foreign steers
as you did not
leaving them where they fell
dead for nothing, to rot

     as you laughed in your sherry
     from porches and doors
     washed white with your joke
     that we seemed so satisfied
     with what you left

and nothing you can do
will stop us
as we re-make
your weapons into charms,
send flying back to you the bullets.

See
we are strong,
we who are so small
we survive unseen;
hear
our beautiful songs
building from the hills
like thunderheads;

watch
the children we weave
from wire bales and string,
from bottles and bullets,
from steer guts and borders—
See, Pahana,
how we nest
in your ruins.

Pahana (Hopi)—Whiteman

Language

Incessant, pushing for the struggle
of re-generation
    one hurricane
replaces another
just when the island has been rejuvenated

Living in kaleidoscope cities
urban twisted metal sculptures
piles of moving fabric
& hair
all that hair, braided together
like a downtown skyline
woven through towers
with a one-two break-beat

Even these buildings have rhythm
metalworker songs
& saw blade scratches
    take them as a symbol
of our rise-up stance
educate our children for a second chance

Ain't no three strikes in the world I live in

We speak forgiveness
like giraffe tongues
long & ready to unravel

We speak change
in the language of the playground
the dialect of freeways and b-ball courts
We understand that nothing happens without a declaration
        even independence

So we declare this place our home
and push forward with those who push
& move past the ones whose feet can catch no rhythm
whose lives remain cemented in a history
Unchanged   plagued by the parliament of greed

We declare an eastern expansion
a manifest where the west must rest
& leave its tired self behind

We speak ancestor codes of
handshake body language
& "brother I got your back"

We speak cross-generational tongues
of bilingual *I love yous*
& grand-parental recognition

We break things down to the critical
so that each generation can link to the next
		without severance

We speak in the grand tongue of humanity
a language without saliva
an underground dialect
whose code will be deciphered
and whose only script will read:

"Daughter, son, we're ready for you."

Equality

This sun-sponsored morning
Sweeps through tasseled grasses
    and spread-armed trees
Into expectant nooks and corners
    of a hawk-eyed landscape
Not concerned about which of us
Is burdened from memories
We've carried through our nation's scalded history
Where you were star-crossed
      if you came out
Black or red or yellow
      if your god
Was not like theirs.
Observe children, their small sounds
Splashing laughing.
        And listen to the dead.
        We may still be able to boost
    our frayed limbs into the sky
On fickle winds that spread
Passions along dark folds
    of clouds
Designed to expose the ashes
      along with the truth.

SANDRA MARÍA ESTEVES

Blanket Weaver

weaver
weave us a song of many threads

weave us a red of fire and blood
that taste of sweet plum
fishing around the memories of the dead
following a scent wounded
our spines bleeding with pain

weave us a red of passion
that beats wings against a smoky cloud
and forces motion into our lungs

weave us a song
of yellow and gold and life itself
that lights a way through wild growth
burned in pain
aged with steady conviction
with bunions callouses and leathered hides

weave us into the great magnetic center
pulling your fingers into topaz canyons
a single lonely web glitters like a flash of thunder
your thumb feeling into my womb
placing sweatseeds of floral honey
into continuous universal suspension

weave us a song of red and yellow
and brown
that holds the sea and the sky in its skin
that holds the bird and mountain in its voice
that builds upon our graves a home
for injustice fear oppression abuse and disgrace
and upon these fortifications
of strength unity and direction

weave us a song to hold us
when the wind blows so cold to make our children wail
submerged in furious ice
a song pure and raw
that burns paper
and attacks the colorless venom stalking hidden
in the petal soft sweetness of the black night

weave us a rich round black that lives
in the eyes of our warrior child
and feeds our mouths with moon breezes
with rhythms interflowing
through all spaces of existence
a black that holds the movement of eternity

weave us a song for our bodies to sing

weave us a song of many threads
that will dance with the colors of our people
and cover us with the warmth of peace.

EVERETT HOAGLAND

What It Is/What It Ain't

"... of ... historical hangovers
... literary cornflakes ... university corners
of tailored intellect & universal anesthesia ..."
—from "On" by Bob Kaufman

here's to those
who colored history
with sex race blood
encoded us in the U.S.
& elsewhere

called themselves white
called other
people black red yellow mulat-
toes negroes mestizos—you name it

those who still
rent spent minds
by paying muddled middle
men & women to buy into
today's all
right with the right-
wing diversion of consciousness
"movement" they have
called *multiculturalism* have
called *diversity*

an all fluff & no stuff
in
insubstantial apolitical
subversion of
substitute for
anti-racism for

real change for chump change
given to neatly tied & bowed
new hanker-
chief head-n.i.c. overseers

who in turn push it
on us covered with
the mass printed
multicolored dots
on an airtight wonder

bread wrapper
for some cotton
candy semblance
of the staff of life mass
starved folk fight & die for

what should a poet write about all
the bread cooled out sopped up
bloods & other "minorities"
are making off with
getting off on
this new

offsetting
of our ongoing
right on collective
human rights struggles

with this window dressing diversity
bag that is about as universal
as a eurocentric university
lit crit scene?

nixed "mixed" blood
cop baton beaten
bop beat
poet
bob

kaufman might say
read "On"

Attitude Adjustment

Yo', Dr. and Ms. C.E.O.,
what's goin' on?
"Multiculturalism?" Well and good.
But don't stop there! How does that empower

us down in the 'hood? How
is that an end? Just
like you did back in the day,
you say you care.

You provide opportunity for us
to fete our films, our food, to parade
our style, flair, our dance and ethnic hair.
Like back in the Harlem Renaissance

or, not too long ago,
when we wore dashiki
and 'fro. Yeah, it's all good
for any generation.

Even so, it's no substitute for
political self-
determination. Thought we learned
it ain't nothin' but a means

to an end, an amends, interlude. Other-
wise we are left behind
without institutional power
or our own authority, with
only our color-
ful neo-Negritude, Latinotude,
Arabitude, Indianitude,
Asianitude—
and an ongoin' attitude!!

Post Election Sequence

Look! The harvest time comes in the fall
of the year, when the leaves fly off the branches
red as can be, and ginkgo trees turn into sunlight.
Pumpkins and apples, bright wheat and corn.
So much abundance, color, nourishment, joy!

The harvest time comes in the early years in this
        century, when feet of many colors,
worn smooth from marching, rest for a while;
and when souls who resisted humiliation
for years stand up straight again for a while;
and when eyes whose tears before the lynching
tree and broken ballot box are finished weeping
for a while;
and they all bring out the sharp sickle of their joy
        and reap the sweet yield of harvest day.

The harvest time comes today,
when the week's warm sun and cold rain,
joys, worries, ecstasies and sorrows,
emotional somersaulting, and exhaustion
finally make it through the finale of ads and signs,
        painful commercials and daily wincing

into the bright clearing of this moment,
where the quietness is neither red or blue
or even purple, but where now we reap
some abundant silence to feed us for a while.

MARTA I. VALENTÍN

The Resting Place Makes the Journey Doable

The Spirit moves
The Spirit moves us
The Spirit moves our bodies, our souls
    Our hearts, our hands
       Our feet, our heads
Our thoughts . . .

The World moves us to prayer, to peace,
to live a spiritual life that promotes justice
sustains itself
Is multicultural
anti-oppressive
A spirituality that is the wholeness of life
A wholeness handed down from generation
to generation by ancestors that keep watch,
walk with us, dream with us, push us
into tomorrow
by pulling us out of yesterday
knowing that our continued journey
is never going to be perfect
is always going to demand resting places

The title of this poem is from the words of Dr. Fredrica Harris Thompsett

to make the journey doable
to carry us full circle from beginnings to endings
and back again
and again.

Spirit moves us to be flexible, spontaneous,
like a dance be willing to be led
from God to God
like a song lift our voices in harmony
Praise Her, Praise Him
Celebrate you and me
Thou and them
Make ritual with it, build community of it,
For all relations matter
intersect, interconnect,
intercede and intermingle,
intervolve and interchange, and are
intertribal . . .

May all nations rise up together
and with FireSpirit burn to ashes
the Great Anger that separates us.

May all nations rise up together
and with WaterSpirit wash away
the Great Shame that drowns us.

May all nations rise up together
and with EarthSpirit bury
the Great Hate that strangles us.

May all nations rise up together
and with AirSpirit blow away
the Great Fear that stops us.

As we leave this resting place today
may we find the rhythm of our own soul
and ever dance to it.

PAULA COLE JONES

Reflections

When Father Time has touched my brow
And beckoned unto me
I'll stop to take a look at how
I reached my destiny

Did I honor those who'd gone before
And the gifts they left behind
Preserved their best forevermore
As the story of mankind

Did I share the burdens of today
Help others learn to cease
To let the negatives outweigh
A life of strength and peace

Did I work for those who've yet to come
By doing what I must
Refusing to be led by some
In breaking of the trust

As for the question of my worth
Which I alone must face
I'll know my time upon this earth
Has been a life of grace

Towa

Before communities of strangers settled,
 marking Pueblo boundaries
 and changing the arid
 open landscape forever,
 there were the people of Black Mesa,
 who called themselves Towa.
People whose clear, brown eyes witnessed
 star explosions high above them,
 against a celestial canvas of darkness,
 the Towa were filled with mystery,
  wonder
   and reverence
    for the universe encircling them.
 Reverence gave birth to ritual,
 celebration wove ceremony
 into songs that blanketed the village
 with life-giving spirit.
Planting nourishment for the children of Puye,
 with steady handwork,
 bedding seeds of corn,
  squash
   and beans.
Drum beats pounded upward,
 introducing a new season's fertile ground.
 Nimble fingers pressing seedlings into earth beds,

Digging,
  planting,
    covering and smoothing
      in perpetual motion,
        connecting each Towa
          to the cycle of plant life.
From the heavens, to the rain-drenched earth beds,
  to the seedlings ripened into colored corn.
From the harvest to the Corn Dance.
  Clay-skinned people,
  danced with willowlike movements,
  then melted quietly into waiting earth beds.
  Seedlings creating another
    and yet another of these Towa.
  The plant and human life cycle,
    equal in symmetry.
This was before change disrupted night's mystery
  and other world views crowded into Pueblo boundaries
  Now Towa rush to their jobs outside of village walls,
  adapting to standards unlike their own.
  Dressing our clay-skinned bodies
  in image conscious fashion,
  we stroke this new life of comfort.
Yet, somewhere in us,
  persistent sounds surge upward
  reminding us of our life cycles,
    and the innocent wonder
      that is our birthright,
        as children of the Towa.

JOY HARJO

Reconciliation—A Prayer

I
We gather by the shore of all knowledge as peoples who were put here by a god who wanted relatives.

This god was lonely for touch, and imagined herself as a woman, with children to suckle, to sing with—to continue the web of the terrifyingly beautiful cosmos of her womb.

This god became a father who wished for others to walk beside him in the belly of creation.

This god laughed and cried with us as a sister at the sweet tragedy of our predicament—foolish humans—

Or built a fire, as a brother to keep us warm.

This god who grew to love us became our lover, sharing tables of food enough for everyone in this whole world.

II
Oh sun, moon, stars, our other relatives peering at us from the inside of god's house, walk with us as we climb into the next century naked but for the stories we have of each other. Keep us from giving up in this land of nightmares which is also the land of miracles.

We sing our song which we've been promised has no beginning or end.

III

All acts of kindness are lights in the war for justice.

IV

We gather up these strands broken from the web of life. They shiver with our love, as we call them the names of our relatives and carry them to our home made of the four directions and sing:

Of the south, where we feasted and were given new clothes.

Of the west, where we gave up the best of us to the stars as food for the battle.

Of the north, where we cried because we were forsaken by our dreams.

Of the east, because returned to us is the spirit of all that we love.

Acknowledgments

On behalf of all who read this anthology, I thank the poets whose voices are captured in these pages—their expansive insights and artistry are gifts that help us acknowledge the ongoing business of building a multicultural society. Thanks to all of the writers who responded to the invitation.

I thank Dr. William E. Cross for writing the Foreword. His book, *Shades of Black: Diversity in African-American Identity*, and his theory of "Nigrescence" were breakthroughs in shifting the way that people understand black identity. I am also thankful to Dr. Robert Freeman, retired psychologist and ten-year participant in A Dialogue on Race & Ethnicity (ADORE), who introduced me to racial identity development models. I acknowledge Regine Tallyrand for giving us a presentation on Dr. Janet Helm's work on white racial identity development. Since then, racial identity development has been a mainstay in my work and a great inspiration throughout this project. I thank Dr. Leon Spencer for helping expose me and many others to cutting edge voices in cross-cultural studies. I thank Rev. Tracey Robinson-Harris and Rev. William Sinkford for their mentorship and friendship.

I thank the DRUUMM (Diverse & Revolutionary Unitarian Universalist Multicultural Ministries) community for deepening my love and understanding of the multicultural community, and the Unitarian Universalist Association for its ongoing commitment to addressing racism and oppression.

I am lucky to be married to a world explorer, Dr. A. José Jones, who created an entrée to world travel through scuba diving that enticed me and many African Americans to plunge into cultural pasts and enrich our present world views. I thank my daughter, Kendall, for her love and support.

Special thanks go to Skinner House Books for making this publication possible and to Fred Courtright for helping to connect us with a talented pool of writers—also to Mary Benard and Marshall Hawkins of Skinner House for their expertise and ongoing dialogue as this book took shape.

Finally, I extend my appreciation to Christine Toll for reading the manuscript with a sharp eye, and being a sounding board and a friend.